Facts About the Harpy Eagle

By Lisa Strattin

© 2021 Lisa Strattin

FREE BOOK

FREE FOR ALL SUBSCRIBERS

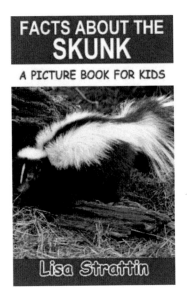

LisaStrattin.com/Subscribe-Here

BOX SET

- **FACTS ABOUT THE POISON DART FROGS**
- **FACTS ABOUT THE THREE TOED SLOTH**
- **FACTS ABOUT THE RED PANDA**
- **FACTS ABOUT THE SEAHORSE**
- **FACTS ABOUT THE PLATYPUS**
- **FACTS ABOUT THE REINDEER**
- **FACTS ABOUT THE PANTHER**
- **FACTS ABOUT THE SIBERIAN HUSKY**

LisaStrattin.com/BookBundle

Facts for Kids Picture Books by Lisa Strattin

Little Blue Penguin, Vol 92

Chipmunk, Vol 5

Frilled Lizard, Vol 39

Blue and Gold Macaw, Vol 13

Poison Dart Frogs, Vol 50

Blue Tarantula, Vol 115

African Elephants, Vol 8

Amur Leopard, Vol 89

Sabre Tooth Tiger, Vol 167

Baboon, Vol 174

Sign Up for New Release Emails Here

LisaStrattin.com/subscribe-here

COVER IMAGE

www.flickr.com/photos/rulenumberone2/49920277028

ADDITIONAL IMAGES

https://www.flickr.com/photos/vil_sandi/30496198503

https://www.flickr.com/photos/cuatrok77/25820897512

https://www.flickr.com/photos/cuatrok77/10918252366

https://www.flickr.com/photos/cuatrok77/21571971609

https://www.flickr.com/photos/twobears2/30247437352

https://www.flickr.com/photos/jitze1942/6285021280

https://www.flickr.com/photos/jitze1942/6285020832

https://www.flickr.com/photos/ekilby/6991500211

https://www.flickr.com/photos/cuatrok77/10943386316

https://www.flickr.com/photos/cuatrok77/25641151810

Contents

INTRODUCTION...9

CHARACTERISTICS 11

APPEARANCE 13

LIFE STAGES 15

LIFE SPAN 17

SIZE...19

HABITAT...21

DIET...23

ENEMIES...25

SUITABILITY AS PETS..27

INTRODUCTION

The Harpy Eagle is a large raptor that lives in the trees of the Central American rainforests. In Brazil, it is called the Royal-Hawk.

The Crested Eagle is its most closely related bird.

They are named after the Harpies of Greek Mythology, supposedly with a vulture's body type but a woman's face!

CHARACTERISTICS

The Harpy Eagle is thought to be the largest species of bird in Central America. But since there is a lot of area there, no one is sure that there are not bigger birds somewhere in these forests.

These eagles mate for life!

Their back talons are thick, curved and 5 inches long. They are actually larger than the claws of a Grizzly Bear!

APPEARANCE

On the Harpy Eagle's back and wings, the feathers are black, but those black feathers are white underneath. Their tail has black feathers with 3 gray bands across it on top, but these bands underneath are white. They look striking when you see them fly – with the colors switching from the topside of the feathers and the underside.

They also have a white belly, but a black band runs across their body between their gray head and belly at the top of their chest.

The iris of their eyes can be brown, gray or even red!

LIFE STAGES

The Harpy Eagle, like other Eagles starts out as an egg in the nest. When they first hatch, or come out of the egg, they are referred to as hatchlings. When they first leave the nest (learn to fly) they are called fledglings. As they begin to get older, they are juveniles, then they become adults and able to start their own family.

LIFE SPAN

The Harpy Eagle lives to be 25 to 35 years of age.

SIZE

The wingspan of the Harpy Eagle can be as much as 6.5 feet! This means that from one wingtip to the other is more than the height of most people. You can ask your mom or dad how tall they are, and that will give you an idea of the span of one of these Eagle's wings!

Normally they weigh between 12 and 22 pounds and grow from about 3 feet to 3.5 feet tall. They are VERY BIG!

HABITAT

The Harpy Eagle builds a nest that can be from 90 to 150 feet high off the ground. They build them in high trees over several branches with a clear flight path that will allow them to go to and from their nest swiftly. They use very big sticks to build the nest and it is usually about 5 feet across and 4 feet deep.

You could even lay down in their nest, it's that big and strong!

DIET

The Harpy Eagle is a carnivore. This means that they eat other animals. They will eat monkeys, sloths and opossums, some other birds and even reptiles, like iguanas.

They are fierce hunters!

ENEMIES

The Harpy Eagles are strong, powerful birds that are hunters instead of being hunted. They are considered to be at the "top of the food chain."

This means that they don't have enemies to worry about, because they are able to overtake the other animals in the forest, even those that are larger than themselves.

SUITABILITY AS PETS

Of course, the Harpy Eagle is not a good choice for a house pet. They need lots of space and are aggressive when anything threatens their nest. It would be better to consider a small bird like a Parakeet, if you want a pet. There are some larger birds that you can have as pets too, like Parrots, but even Parrots are WAY SMALLER than a Harpy Eagle.

You might be able to see one of these Eagles in a zoo. You could call your local zoo to see if they have one in a habitat that has been built just for them.

If you travel to the rainforests of Central America someday, you might be able to spot some of these beautiful birds in the wild!

COLOR ME

COLOR ME

COLOR ME

COLOR ME

COLOR ME

Please leave me a review here:

LisaStrattin.com/Review-Vol-393

For more Kindle Downloads Visit Lisa Strattin Author Page on Amazon Author Central

amazon.com/author/lisastrattin

To see upcoming titles, visit my website at LisaStrattin.com– most books available on Kindle!

LisaStrattin.com

FREE BOOK

FOR ALL SUBSCRIBERS – SIGN UP NOW

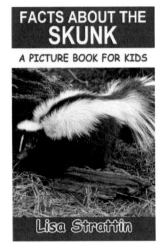

LisaStrattin.com/Subscribe-Here

LisaStrattin.com/Facebook

LisaStrattin.com/YouTube

Made in the USA
Coppell, TX
28 November 2024

41195198R00026